SCHOLASTIC
News
Nonfiction Readers

A Turtle Hatchling Grows Up

by
Pam Zollman

Children's Press®
A Division of Scholastic Inc.
New York Toronto London Auckland Sydney
Mexico City New Delhi Hong Kong
Danbury, Connecticut

These content vocabulary word builders
are for grades 1-2.

Consultant:
Dr. Dale Madison
Professor, Binghamton University
Binghamton, New York

Curriculum Specialist: Linda Bullock
Reading Specialist: Don Curry

Special thanks to the Kansas City Zoo and Omaha's Henry Doorly Zoo

Photo Credits:

Photographs © 2005: Animals Animals: 21 top right (Patricia Caulfield), 16 (George H. Huey), 23 top left (Marie Read), 23 bottom left (Viola's Photo Visions, Inc.); Brian Kenney: 6; Corbis Images: 5 bottom right, 9 top (Darrell Gulin), cover center inset, 21 bottom left (Kevin Schafer), 23 bottom right (Chase Swift), cover right inset, 2, 20 right center, 21 top left (Kennan Ward), 23 top right (Lawson Wood); Dembinsky Photo Assoc.: back cover (Jesse Cancelmo), 4 bottom left, 5 top, 7, 14, 15 (A. B. Sheldon); Minden Pictures: 1, 13, 18, 21 center right (Frans Lanting), 17 (Mike Parry), cover background (Norbert Wu); National Geographic Image Collection: 11 (Brian J. Skerry), 4 top, 12 (Steve Winter), cover left inset, 20 bottom right (Reinhard Dirscherl/Bilderberg), 19, 20 top left (Rudiger Lehnen), 20 center left (Alexis Rosenfeld); Visuals Unlimited/Ken Lucas: 4 bottom right, 5 bottom left, 9 bottom.

Book Design: Simonsays Design!

Library of Congress Cataloging-in-Publication Data

Zollman, Pam.
    A turtle hatchling grows up / by Pam Zollman.
        p. cm. — (Scholastic news nonfiction readers)
    Includes bibliographical references and index.
    ISBN 0-516-24948-7 (lib. bdg.)
    1. Turtles—Development—Juvenile literature. I. Title. II. Series.
    QL666.C5Z65 2005
    597.92'139—dc22

                                                    2005003294

1 2 3 4 5 6 7 8 9 10 R 14 13 12 11 10 09 08 07 06 05

Scholastic 6/14/06 $12.60

CONTENTS

WORD HUNT

Look for these words as you read. They will be in **bold**.

egg
(eg)

hatchling
(**hach**-ling)

shell
(shel)

4

egg tooth
(eg tooth)

hatch
(hach)

tortoise
(**tor**-tuhss)

turtle
(**tur**-tuhl)

Hatchlings!

Have you ever seen a baby **turtle**?

It is called a **hatchling**.

Baby **tortoises** look like baby turtles. They are called hatchlings, too.

tortoise hatchling

This turtle hatchling is coming out of an egg.

Tortoises are turtles that live on land.

A tortoise has a high, round **shell**.

Turtles that live in water have a low, flat shell.

shell

This turtle's shell is low and flat.

This tortoise's shell is high and round.

shell

Sea turtles spend most of their time in the water.

Female sea turtles swim to the same beach every year.

They go there to lay eggs.

Look at this sea turtle swim!

This sea turtle mother digs a hole in the sand.

She lays **eggs** in the hole.

She covers the eggs with sand.

Then she goes back to the water.

eggs

This sea turtle mother is digging a hole. She will lay eggs in it.

The eggs **hatch** in a few months.

The hatchlings have an **egg tooth**.

They use it to open the soft shells of their eggs.

Then the turtles come out.

egg tooth

Look! The turtle hatchling used its egg tooth to open the egg.

Sea turtle hatchlings go to the water.

They eat jellyfish.

Tortoise hatchlings stay on land.

They eat grasses and plants.

tortoise hatchling

These sea turtle hatchlings are going to the water.

All hatchlings look like their parents.

They are just smaller.

It takes years for them to grow up.

sea turtle hatchling

This sea turtle
is grown-up.

A Turtle Hatchling Grows Up!

1····

A mother
sea turtle
swims to
a beach.

2···

She digs a hole.
Then she lays eggs.

3····

She covers the eggs
with sand.

7 Now the sea turtle is grown-up.

6 The turtle hatchling is growing! It eats jellyfish, turtle grass, and other things.

5 Now the turtle hatchling goes to the water.

4 Look! An egg is hatching. It's a sea turtle hatchling.

YOUR NEW WORDS

egg (eg) a round or oval shell in which a baby grows

egg tooth (eg tooth) a sharp tooth that a hatchling uses to open its egg

hatch (hach) to break out of an egg

hatchling (**hach**-ling) a baby animal that hatches from an egg

shell (shel) a hard or soft covering

tortoise (**tor**-tuhss) a turtle that lives on land

turtle (**tur**-tuhl) a kind of reptile that lives on land and in water

THESE ANIMALS HAVE SHELLS, TOO!

armadillo

crab

scallop

snail

INDEX

FIND OUT MORE

Book:

See Through: Reptiles, by Steve Parker (Running Press Kids, 2003)

Website:

http://www.tortoise-tracks.org/gopherus/lifecycle.html

MEET THE AUTHOR:

Pam Zollman is the award-winning author of short stories, articles, and books for kids. She is the author of other Life Cycles books in the *Scholastic News Nonfiction Readers* series. She lives in rural Pennsylvania and once had a pet turtle.